GOOD NEWS

The Gospel from Genesis to Revelation

9 studies
for individuals or groups

Jack Kuhatschek

With Notes for Leaders

T0338950

Scripture Union is an international Christian charity working with churches in more than 130 countries.

Thank you for purchasing this book. Any profits from this book support SU in England and Wales to bring the good news of Jesus Christ to children, young people and families and to enable them to meet God through the Bible and prayer.

Find out more about our work and how you can get involved at:

www.scriptureunion.org.uk (England and Wales)
www.suscotland.org.uk (Scotland)
www.suni.co.uk (Northern Ireland)
www.scriptureunion.org (USA)
www.su.org.au (Australia)

ISBN 978 1 78506 656 6

First published in the United States by InterVarsity Press 2017.
© Jack Kuhatschek

This edition published in the United Kingdom © Scripture Union 2017.

Scripture quotations, unless otherwise indicated, are taken from the Holy Bible, New International Version. Copyright © 1973, 1978, 1984 by International Bible Society. Anglicisation copyright © 1979, 1984, 1989. Used by permission of Hodder and Stoughton Limited.

British Library Cataloguing-in-Publication data: a catalogue record for this book is available from the British Library.

Printed in Malta by Melita Press

Image credit: golero/iStock by Getty Images

Contents

Getting the Most Out of
Good News

For centuries people had been aware of mysterious lines covering 190 square miles in the Nazca Desert in southern Peru. In 1553 Pedro Cieza de León wrote that they might have been ancient trail markers. But in 1940 Paul Kosok, a historian from Long Island University, flew over the lines and realized that one was in the shape of a giant bird. He was soon joined in his research by Maria Reiche, a German mathematician and archaeologist, who studied the lines for the remainder of her life. We now know that these drawings—the largest of which spans nearly nine hundred feet—include images of a hummingbird, a condor, a whale, a spider, a monkey, and hundreds of other animal and human figures. Yet the meaning of the lines could only be discerned far above the desert floor.

In a similar way, the full contours of the gospel can only be seen and appreciated when we scan the biblical horizon from Genesis to Revelation. That explains, in part, why God wrote such a lengthy book rather than a gospel tract. Of course there is great benefit in brief summaries of the good news, such as "The Four Spiritual Laws"—I became a Christian the night someone shared such a booklet with me. Yet if we want to recapture the spirit of the two disciples on the road to Emmaus, when their hearts burned with excitement and passion within them, then we'll need to begin with Moses and all the prophets to understand what was said in all the Scriptures concerning Jesus and his reason for coming.

In recent years a number of books have been written about the gospel. These include *The King Jesus Gospel* by Scot McKnight, *Simply Good News* by N. T. Wright, *The Explicit Gospel* by Matt Chandler, and *What Is the Gospel?* by Greg Gilbert. Several authors have claimed that evangelicals teach a truncated gospel—one that explains personal salvation but omits the incredibly broad scope of what God has done, is doing, and will do in the future to reconcile all things to himself through Jesus Christ.

I'm hoping that this LifeGuide will not only explain what we must do to be saved but also help you understand the background and far-reaching implications of the good news we have believed.

Suggestions for Individual Study

1. As you begin each study, pray that God will speak to you through his Word.

2. Read the introduction to the study and respond to the personal reflection question or exercise. This is designed to help you focus on God and on the theme of the study.

3. Each study deals with a particular passage so that you can delve into the author's meaning in that context. Read and reread the passage to be studied. The questions are written using the language of the New International Version, so you may wish to use that version of the Bible. The New Revised Standard Version is also recommended.

4. This is an inductive Bible study, designed to help you discover for yourself what Scripture is saying. The study includes three types of questions. *Observation* questions ask about the basic facts: who, what, when, where, and how. *Interpretation* questions delve into the meaning of the passage. *Application* questions help you discover the implications of the text for growing in Christ. These three keys unlock the treasures of Scripture.

Write your answers to the questions in the spaces provided or in a personal journal. Writing can bring clarity and deeper understanding of yourself and of God's Word.

5. It might be good to have a Bible dictionary handy. Use it to look up any unfamiliar words, names or places.

6. Use the prayer suggestion to guide you in thanking God for what you have learned and to pray about the applications that have come to mind.

7. You may want to go on to the suggestion under "Now or Later," or you may want to use that idea for your next study.

Suggestions for Members of a Group Study

1. Come to the study prepared. Follow the suggestions for individual study mentioned above. You will find that careful preparation will greatly enrich your time spent in group discussion.

2. Be willing to participate in the discussion. The leader of your group will not be lecturing. Instead, he or she will be encouraging the members of the group to discuss what they have learned. The leader will be asking the questions that are found in this guide.

3. Stick to the topic being discussed. Your answers should be based on the verses that are the focus of the discussion and not on outside authorities such as commentaries or speakers. These studies focus on a particular passage of Scripture. Only rarely should you refer to other portions of the Bible. This allows for everyone to participate in in-depth study on equal ground.

4. Be sensitive to the other members of the group. Listen attentively when they describe what they have learned. You may be surprised by their insights! Each question assumes a variety of answers. Many questions do not have "right" answers, particularly questions that aim at meaning or application. Instead the questions push us to explore the passage more thoroughly.

When possible, link what you say to the comments of others. Also, be affirming whenever you can. This will encourage some of the more hesitant members of the group to participate.

5. Be careful not to dominate the discussion. We are sometimes so eager to express our thoughts that we leave too little opportunity for others to respond. By all means participate! But allow others to also.

6. Expect God to teach you through the passage being discussed and through the other members of the group. Pray that you will have an enjoyable and profitable time together, but also that as a result of the study you will find ways that you can take action individually and/or as a group.

7. Remember that anything said in the group is considered confidential and should not be discussed outside the group unless specific permission is given to do so.

8. If you are the group leader, you will find additional suggestions at the back of the guide.

1

Created in His Image

In the Woody Allen movie *Midnight in Paris*, an American screenwriter named Gil is on a holiday in France with his fiancée and her family. Even though the beauties of present-day Paris surround him, Gil wishes he could have visited in Paris during the Jazz Age of the 1920s when the city hosted such literary giants as F. Scott Fitzgerald, Ernest Hemingway, and Gertrude Stein.

While on a stroll one evening, Gil is transported at the stroke of midnight back to the 1920s and is thrilled to meet not only Fitzgerald, Hemingway, and Stein but also Pablo Picasso, Salvador Dali, Cole Porter, and many others. Gil soon falls in love with Picasso's lover, Adriana, but is shocked to discover that she doesn't appreciate Gil's beloved Jazz Age. She wishes she had lived during another period known as La Belle Époque, between 1871 and 1914, when the Moulin Rouge was the center of cultural activity.

By the end of the movie, the two lovers depart from each other, knowing that they each long to live in a time other than their own.

GROUP DISCUSSION. If you could travel back in time to either one of your favorite periods of history or one of the best times of your life, what would you choose, and why?

PERSONAL REFLECTION. Why do you think people often feel nostalgia for either "the good old days" or for some special time in their past?

In Genesis 1:26–2:25 we'll look back at the dawn of time, when God not only delighted in his creation, declaring it "very good," but also in the man and woman he had created in his image and likeness. We will never understand the gospel until we realize that the sinful world around and within us is neither the original nor natural state God intended, which explains why we long for a time that is different from the one we have always known. *Read Genesis 1:26–2:25.*

---

1. On the sixth day, the culmination of God's creation, God creates humankind. In what ways do the man and woman differ from the rest of creation?

---

2. What do you think it means to be created in God's image and likeness (vv. 26-27; see also Genesis 5:3; 2 Corinthians 3:17-18)?

---

3. Why is it important to realize that there was a time when God declared that everything he had created was "very good"?

4. Read Genesis 2:4-25. Many scholars believe that these verses are not a so-called "second creation story" but rather an expanded explanation of the creation of humanity. What details in this passage support that perspective?

_____

5. When we describe any place today as a veritable "Garden of Eden," we assume that it has incredible beauty. What features stand out in this passage about the garden home of the original couple?

_____

6. What responsibilities, provisions, and restrictions does God give Adam in verses 8-17?

Why do you think the Lord planted a tree in the middle of the garden that had fruit the couple was forbidden to eat (v. 17)?

_____

7. Although the Lord had declared the whole of creation "very good" in Genesis 1, this chapter states that something is "not good" (v. 18). How does the responsibility of naming the animals help Adam see his needs more clearly (vv. 19-20)?

8. In what ways is marriage a portrait of what it means (in part) to be created in the image of God (vv. 21-25; see also Ephesians 5:31-32)?

---

9. When we discuss the gospel with those around us, why is it important to begin with the original goodness of creation and humanity rather than with the problem of sin?

Thank the Lord for creating us in his image and likeness so we can know and relate to him—the infinite God of the universe.

Now or Later

Take time today to appreciate the goodness of God's creation by noticing the beauty and intricacy of the world around you.

2

The Fall of Humanity

Genesis 3

In an essay titled "But Man Fell on Earth," pastor and author Helmut Thielicke tells about visiting a group of young soldiers on the battlefield on the day when one of their friends had died. The boys gathered around the pastor "almost like chicks round a hen." He tried to speak words of comfort to them but felt utterly helpless. He writes:

> But then the thing happened that accounts for my relating this incident at all. On my way home the moonlight lay upon the quiet valley, the white flowers of the trees shimmered in this soft light, and an unspeakable peace and stillness rested upon the landscape. The world was "like some quiet room, where wrapt in still soft gloom, we sleep away the daylight's sorrow."
>
> I mention this, not to be romantic or to gain a sentimental effect, but rather because for me this hour was a parable of the dark threshold which, the account of the Fall says, man has crossed. Before me lay the seemingly whole and healthy world of a springtime night. But in that moment its very peace was like a stab of pain. For I knew that the peace of nature is delusive, and that I had

just spoken, encompassed by a sea of blossoms, with boys whose eyes were filled with dread even though they bravely swallowed their tears.*

GROUP DISCUSSION. Describe a time in your life when "the seemingly whole and healthy world" was disrupted by pain, sorrow, or tragedy.

PERSONAL REFLECTION. Even though we live in a world filled with the beauty of nature, how is Thielicke correct when he writes the "the peace of nature is delusive"?

In this session we will look at "the dark threshold which, the account of the Fall says, man has crossed." *Read Genesis 3.*

---

1. Although the New Testament identifies the serpent in Genesis 3 as Satan (Revelation 12:9; 20:2), here he is merely described as "more crafty than any of the wild animals the LORD God had made" (v. 1). How do the serpent's question and the woman's response differ from what the Lord actually said (Genesis 3:1-3; 2:16-17)?

---

2. What is the serpent trying to insinuate by his twisting of God's words (v. 1)?

What significance, if any, do you see in the woman's inaccurate recounting of God's commands (vv. 2-3)?

3. How does the serpent assault God's character in verses 4-5?

What impact do you think the serpent hopes to have on the woman?

---

4. Why does Satan try to convince us that God doesn't have our best interests in mind?

---

5. After her conversation with the serpent, how does the woman see the fruit of the tree in a new light (v. 6; see also 1 John 2:16)?

---

6. How do the couple's responses after their sin (vv. 7-8) contrast with the closing verse of chapter 2?

---

7. What four pointed questions does the Lord ask the couple (vv. 9-13)?

How do they seek to avoid taking responsibility for their sin?

8. Why are we tempted today to blame anyone but ourselves for our moral failings?

---

9. What are the far-reaching consequences of sin for the serpent (vv. 14-15), the woman (v. 16), and the man (vv. 17-24)?

---

10. Throughout history, people have claimed that the presence of evil in the world means that God must either be all-powerful but not good, or else good but not all-powerful. How does Genesis 3 challenge that idea?

Take time to confess your sins to the Lord, thanking him for the forgiveness we have through the gospel.

Now or Later

As you read about the national or international news this week, take time to reflect on events that underscore the fact that sin has entered the world.

---

*Helmut Thielicke, "But Man Fell on Earth," *Christianity Today*, March 4, 1977, 15; adapted from Thielicke's sermon collection *How the World Began* (London: James Clarke, 1964).

3

The Call of Abram

Genesis 12:1-9

In 1885 seven university students, who were later dubbed the "Cambridge Seven," shocked the people of England and Scotland by leaving behind their lives of privilege and comfort in order to become missionaries in China. Before departing, they conducted a farewell tour on campuses throughout England and Scotland, urging other students to follow their example by committing their lives completely to Christ. Even Queen Victoria was given a copy of a booklet containing their testimonies. All seven men went to China and spent many years as missionaries in that country, and three of them remained there until the end of their lives. Their story was published as *The Evangelization of the World* and was distributed to every YMCA and YWCA throughout the British Empire and the United States.

GROUP DISCUSSION. Why do you think some Christians believe that Jesus is their key to health, wealth, and success, while others are willing to give their lives in sacrificial service?

PERSONAL REFLECTION. Think of a specific time when you were willing to make a personal sacrifice in order to follow Christ. What were the costs and benefits of that sacrifice?

In Genesis 12 we will look at the call of Abram, who was later named Abraham, and discover why he is such an important part of the gospel narrative. *Read Genesis 12:1-9.*

---

1. What is Abram giving up to follow the Lord's command (v. 1)?

---

2. What specific promises does the Lord make to Abram (vv. 2-3; see also Genesis 17:3-8)?

---

3. What do you think the Lord means when he says that "all peoples on earth will be blessed through you" (v. 3; see also Galatians 3:14, 29)?

---

4. By the time of Jesus, the people of Israel had developed an "us versus them" mentality, viewing the Jews as God's chosen people and the Gentile nations as "dogs." How had they lost the purpose and extent of God's promises?

5. In what ways do we have a too limited view of God's vision for the world?

6. Verse 4 tells us that "Abram was seventy-five years old when he set out from Harran." How did his advanced age underscore the faith he needed to believe and obey the Lord (see also Genesis 15:2-6)?

7. How would the presence of the Canaanites in the land (vv. 6-7) require additional faith on Abram's part?

8. Do you have difficulty trusting God when your circumstances seem to run counter to his promises? Explain.

9. In what ways is Abram's faith evident as he travels from Shechem (v. 6) to Bethel (v. 8) to the Negev (v. 9)?

---

10. How does this passage help you to understand the gospel's connection to the promises made to Abram?

Pray that God would enable you to see and embrace his vision for blessing all the nations of the earth.

Now or Later

Take time this week to pray for believers throughout the world, especially those facing persecution for their faith. Pray too for those who have never heard the good news about Jesus Christ.

4

The Law of Moses

Deuteronomy 6

In the movie *City Slickers* a man named Mitch (played by Billy Crystal) and two of his buddies are having a midlife crisis, so they decide to go on two-week vacation out West, driving cattle from New Mexico to Colorado. There they meet a no-nonsense cowboy named Curly (played by Jack Palance), who begins teaching them not only about cattle but also about life itself.

During one memorable scene Curly asks Mitch, "Do you know what the secret of life is? This." [he holds up one finger]

Mitch: Your finger?

Curly: One thing. Just one thing. You stick to that and the rest don't mean s---.

Mitch: But, what is the "one thing"?

Curly: That's what you have to find out.

GROUP DISCUSSION. Do you agree with Curly that the secret of life can be reduced to one thing? Why or why not?

PERSONAL REFLECTION. What one thing has given you the greatest focus and clarity in life?

In Deuteronomy 6 Moses tells the people of Israel what it truly means to serve the Lord. *Read Deuteronomy 6.*

1. According to verses 1-3, what do you think it meant for Israel to "fear the LORD"?

How do these verses reveal the beneficial nature of God's covenant with Israel?

---

2. The Hebrew word for "hear" is *shema*, so verse 4 is known by Jewish people as the Shema, and it is recited by Orthodox Jews morning and night. As Israel entered the land of Canaan, why was it important for them to know that God is "one"?

---

3. Jesus referred to verse 5 as "the first and greatest commandment" (Matthew 22:37-40) and said that when it is joined with the second command ("love your neighbor as yourself") they summarize "all the Law and the Prophets." How could two commands possibly summarize all of the others?

Why is it important for us today to realize that all of God's commands have this overarching purpose and goal?

4. How was God's law supposed to permeate every aspect of Israel's daily life (vv. 6-9)?

5. What temptations will Israel face when they live in the Promised Land, and why (vv. 10-19)?

What are the clear consequences of their obedience or disobedience?

6. Massah (v. 16, which means "testing") refers to the place in the wilderness where Israel tested the Lord by demanding that he quench their thirst (Exodus 17:1-7). How can either prosperity or hardship become a temptation to us today?

7. Verses 20-25 anticipate a day when children who aren't familiar with the Lord's deliverance of Israel from Egypt ask about the meaning of God's "stipulations, decrees and laws." Why is God's work in the past so relevant to Israel's future— and to ours?

8. In Paul's day some people blamed God's law for both sin and death, but Paul explained that "the law is holy, and the commandment is holy, righteous and good" (Romans 7:12). How is the goodness of the law affirmed in Deuteronomy 6?

Why is it important for us today to affirm the goodness of God's commands?

Thank the Lord for the fact that his commands are not arbitrary but rather are grounded in his love for us and others.

Now or Later

Read Psalm 119:97-112, reflecting on the goodness and benefits of God's commands.

5

The Power of Sin

Romans 3:9-20

On July 2, 1881, a man named Charles Guiteau sat at the Baltimore and Potomac Railroad Station in Washington, DC, waiting for President James Garfield to arrive. When he did, Guiteau walked up behind the president and shot him twice in the back with a large-caliber revolver. As Garfield fell to the floor, the assassin cried out "[Chester A.] Arthur is president now!"

When Garfield died eleven weeks later, Guiteau was charged with murder. He was formally indicted on October 14, 1881, but pleaded not guilty. During the trial he sent a letter to Chester Arthur, asking to be set free since he had just increased Arthur's salary by making him president. He also began making plans for a lecture tour after his release and hoped to run for president himself in 1884. Yet in spite of his optimism, the court found him guilty, and he was executed on June 30, 1882.

GROUP DISCUSSION. Although Charles Guiteau may have been insane, why do many sane people assume they have nothing to fear at the Last Judgment?

PERSONAL REFLECTION. When have you been guilty of taking your sin too lightly?

In Romans 1:1–3:8 Paul has been like a prosecuting attorney, making a case that all of humanity—both Jews and Gentiles— have broken God's laws. Now in Romans 3:9-20 the apostle gives us a preview of Judgment Day, allowing us to know the verdict in advance for all who have not had their sins forgiven in Christ. *Read Romans 3:9-20.*

---

1. How do Paul's words in verses 9-12 indicate the all-inclusive impact of sin?

---

2. There are billions of religious people throughout the world. How can Paul possibly claim therefore that "there is no one who seeks God" (v. 11)?

---

3. How do you deal with the tension between Paul's words "there is no one who does good, not even one" (v. 12) and our perception that some people are good, kind, and just?

---

4. How does Paul use the various parts of our bodies in verses 13-18 to describe the pervasive impact of sin in our lives?

5. A number of years ago Dr. Karl Menninger wrote a book titled *Whatever Became of Sin?* If sin is such a blatant and dangerous reality, why do you think society tries to deny its existence?

6. What evidence do you see in the world today that confirms Paul's diagnosis of the human condition?

7. Normally, people make every effort to rationalize their behavior and excuse their actions. Why will that response be impossible on the Day of Judgment (v. 19)?

8. Many people imagine that when their good works are weighed in the balance against their sins, they will be acceptable to God. How does Paul clarify in verse 20 what God's law can and cannot do?

9. Jesus described himself as a doctor who came to heal the effects of sin (Matthew 9:12). Why must we accept the Bible's diagnosis of our condition before we can experience healing grace?

Praise God for the fact that he "did not send his Son into the world to condemn the world, but to save the world through him" (John 3:17).

Now or Later
Take time to read Psalm 51, making David's prayer your own.

6

The Gift of Righteousness

Romans 3:21-31

In Dorothy L. Sayers's novel *Strong Poison*, a woman named Harriet Vane has been accused of murdering her lover. The evidence against her at her trial seems overwhelming until Lord Peter Wimsey finds the real killer. At the conclusion of her trial, Miss Vane's lawyer says to the judge:

> A charge has been brought against her, my lord, the very awful charge of murder, and I should like it to be made clear that my client leaves this court without a stain upon her character. . . . This lady must go forth into the world acquitted, not only at this bar, but at the bar of public opinion.

The judge agrees and says to Harriet Vane:

> Prisoner at the bar, the Crown, by unreservedly withdrawing this dreadful charge against you, has demonstrated your innocence in the clearest possible way. After this, nobody will be able to suppose that the slightest imputation rests upon you. . . . The prisoner is discharged without a stain upon her character. Next case.[*]

GROUP DISCUSSION. Imagine that you have been accused of a serious crime punishable by either life in prison or execution. How would you feel if the jury found you not guilty? Explain.

PERSONAL REFLECTION. Think of a time when you were forgiven by someone for a serious offense. How did you feel, and why?

Paul has already proven that we deserve nothing but God's just condemnation on Judgment Day. But in this passage he makes a major shift from law to grace—and that changes everything. *Read Romans 3:21-31.*

---

1. How does the "righteousness of God" that Paul describes in verses 21-24 contrast with the righteousness mentioned in verses 19-20?

---

2. Why is it important to know that this righteousness was not a New Testament invention but rather was testified to by the Law and the Prophets (v. 21)?

---

3. Paul uses three powerful word pictures in verses 24-25. The first is the word *justified* (v. 24), which uses the language of a law court. The Greek word can mean either to be found not guilty or to be "declared righteous" (v. 20). A judge can declare someone not guilty, but how is being "declared righteous" much more than the absence of guilt?

4. The second word picture comes from the word *redemption*, which means to be purchased out of slavery. In what sense were we slaves before Jesus Christ freed us?

---

5. What evidence do you see in society that people do not merely choose to sin but rather are slaves to sin and need to be set free?

---

6. The third word picture is derived from the words *sacrifice of atonement* (v. 25), which look back to the sacrificial system of the Old Testament. On the Day of Atonement blood was sprinkled on the lid of the ark of the covenant in order to satisfy the wrath of God. How did Jesus' sacrificial death satisfy God's wrath?

---

7. How do Paul's three word pictures help you appreciate what Jesus did for us on the cross?

---

8. In verse 26 Paul says that God did all this "so as to be just and the one who justifies those who have faith in Jesus." In what ways do God's justice and his grace intersect at the cross?

9. How does this passage emphasize that righteousness by grace through faith in Christ should keep us from "boasting" (v. 27)?

---

10. In Paul's day some claimed that righteousness by faith "apart from the law" (v. 21) would "nullify the law" (v. 31). On the contrary, how does righteousness by faith "uphold the law" (v. 31)?

Thank God for the many ways he has delivered us from sin. Tell him how much you appreciate the gift of righteousness he has given you.

Now or Later

In Romans 3:21-31 Paul is describing what Jesus' death on the cross accomplished. Take time now or later to read one or more of the crucifixion accounts, which are found in the following passages: Matthew 27:27-56; Mark 15:16-41; Luke 23:26-49; John 19:1-37. Also make a list of three people you know who need the good news about Jesus. Begin praying for an opportunity to talk with them about your faith.

---

*Dorothy L. Sayers, *Strong Poison* (New York: HarperCollins, 2012), 280.

7

Transformed
by the Spirit

2 Corinthians 3:7-18

When I was in sixth grade, we studied monarch butterflies, carefully learning how to draw and label each of their parts. But the most exciting lesson we learned was about the miracle of metamorphosis, where an ugly caterpillar is transformed into a beautiful butterfly.

As you know, the caterpillar hangs upside down, attached to a leaf or twig. Then it forms a chrysalis, and the miraculous transformation is hidden from our eyes until about ten days later when a magnificent butterfly emerges. Metamorphosis is one of the most incredible displays of change in the natural world.

GROUP DISCUSSION. What other remarkable examples of transformation can you think of from the natural world?

PERSONAL REFLECTION. What personal changes would you most like to experience?

Second Corinthians 3 claims that every Christian is going through a spiritual metamorphosis. We begin life as sinful humans who are totally incapable of loving God and others the way he desires. But when we put our faith in Christ, God promises that someday we will emerge from our spiritual chrysalises as pure and radiant as Jesus himself. *Read 2 Corinthians 3:7-18.*

1. The old covenant (v. 14) was given through Moses and the new covenant (v. 6) through Jesus Christ. What contrasts does Paul make in verses 7-11 between the old and new covenants?

2. According to Paul, why did Moses put a veil over his face after being in the presence of God (vv. 7, 13)?

3. In what sense was a veil also over the hearts of the Israelites in Paul's day (vv. 14-16)?

4. Whenever Moses went into the presence of God, he removed the veil that covered his face, and he would reflect God's radiant glory (Exodus 34:29-35). How is our experience as Christians similar to and even greater than that of Moses (v. 18)?

5. The word *transformed* in verse 18 is a translation of the Greek *metamorphoō*, from which we also get our word *metamorphosis.* What does it mean to be transformed into the image of the Lord (see also Genesis 1:26-27)?

6. What indication does Paul give that this transformation is progressive rather than instantaneous (v. 18)?

---

7. Why is it important for us to realize that spiritual maturity takes time?

---

8. How does Paul emphasize in this passage that our spiritual transformation is a miraculous work of God and not merely the result of human effort?

---

9. Some people in Paul's day—and even today—claim that the gospel can encourage immorality. How does this passage reveal the empty nature of that claim?

Pray that God's Spirit will enable you to cooperate with him in your spiritual metamorphosis.

Now or Later

Even though our spiritual transformation is a miraculous work of God, the spiritual disciplines of prayer, Bible study, and fellowship can stimulate our growth in Christ. In what ways are you taking advantage of these disciplines?

8

The Resurrection

In C. S. Lewis's children's book *The Lion, the Witch, and the Wardrobe*, Aslan the lion voluntarily offers his life in exchange for Edmund's. As the lion makes his way toward the hill where the execution will take place, the witch's evil minions bind him, shave off his beautiful mane, and muzzle him. After they've mocked and spat on the great lion, the crowd drags him onto a stone table. As the witch raises her knife to strike the fatal blow, she says to Aslan, "Understand that you have given me Narnia forever, you have lost your own life and you have not saved his. In that knowledge, despair and die."

Every time my wife and I read this account, we are so caught up in the sadness and tragedy of the event that we must reassure ourselves that it's not the end of the story!

GROUP DISCUSSION. Many people believe that death is a natural part of the life cycle. But from a biblical perspective, how is death unnatural?

PERSONAL REFLECTION. When you think of heaven, do you imagine having a body? Why or why not?

Many Christians today have a Platonic understanding of the gospel that saves our "souls" but gives little thought to the resurrection of the body. In this passage Paul gives a concise summary of the gospel he preaches and emphasizes the crucial importance of the resurrection. *Read 1 Corinthians 15:1-33.*

1. In verse 1 Paul says, "Now, brothers and sisters, I want to remind you of the gospel." How do the words "I preached," "you received," and "you have taken your stand" convey the very specific nature of that gospel (vv. 1-2)?

2. Why is each phrase below a vital part of the gospel?
- "Christ died for our sins" (v. 3)

- "he was buried" (v. 4)

- "he was raised on the third day" (v. 4)

- "according to the Scriptures" (vv. 3, 4)

3. Why do you think Paul places such great emphasis on Christ's resurrection appearances (vv. 5-11)?

4. According to Paul, "if there is no resurrection of the dead," what logical consequences follow (vv. 12-19, 29-32)?

---

5. The Greek poet Menander wrote, "Let us eat and drink, for tomorrow we die" (v. 32). How do his words make sense if there is no life after death?

---

6. In contrast, what are the benefits of the fact that "Christ has indeed been raised from the dead" (vv. 20-28)?

---

7. Like the Greeks of Paul's day, many Christians believe in the immortality of the soul but give little thought to the resurrection of their physical bodies. Why is this view both insufficient and unbiblical?

8. The famous liberal preacher Harry Emerson Fosdick wrote: "For myself I have come to think with more and more certainty that the appearances of Jesus were of a spiritual sort. . . . Certainly, I cannot make real the idea of an animated body. . . . That sort of thing seems to me impossible to be believed in by modern minds."* In light of this passage, how would you respond to those today who, like Fosdick, do not believe in the bodily resurrection of Jesus?

Praise the Lord for the fact that he cares about all of reality, not just what is "spiritual."

Now or Later

Read 1 Corinthians 15:35-58 this week. What additional insights do these verses give you about the resurrection?

---

*Harry Emerson Fosdick, quoted in Robert Moats Miller, *Harry Emerson Fosdick: Preacher, Pastor, Prophet* (New York: Oxford University Press, 1985), 411.

9

Heaven on Earth

On January 18, 1989, Baptist minister Don Piper collided with a truck that crossed into his lane and he was pronounced dead at the scene. Paramedics covered him with a tarp so that onlookers wouldn't stare at him while they attended to the injuries of others. But during the ninety minutes he was dead, Piper claims that he went to heaven. He writes,

> Everything I saw was bright—the brightest colors my eyes had ever beheld—so powerful that no earthly human could take in this brilliance.
>
> In the midst of that powerful scene, I continued to step closer to the gate and assumed that I would go inside. My friends and relatives were all in front of me, calling, urging, and inviting me to follow.
>
> Then the scene changed. I can explain it only by saying that instead of their being in front of me, they were beside me. I felt that they wanted to walk beside me as I passed through the iridescent gate.
>
> Sometimes people have asked me, "How did you move? Did you walk? Did you float?" I don't know. I just moved along with that welcoming crowd. As we came closer to the gate, the music increased and became even more vivid. It would be like walking up to a glorious event after

hearing the faint sounds and seeing everything from a distance. The closer we got, the more intense, alive, and vivid everything became. Just as I reached the gate, my senses were even more heightened, and I felt deliriously happy.

I paused—I'm not sure why—just outside the gate. I was thrilled at the prospect and wanted to go inside. I knew everything would be even more thrilling than what I had experienced so far. At that very moment I was about to realize the yearning of every human heart.*

GROUP DISCUSSION. When you think of heaven, what images come to mind?

PERSONAL REFLECTION. To what extent do thoughts of heaven have an impact on your life on earth?

In Revelation 21 the apostle John gives us a glimpse of what he calls "a new heaven and a new earth." Although his description is filled with layers of symbolism, the reality behind the symbols express our deepest longings. *Read Revelation 21:1-8.*

1. In early Judaism some believed that God would renew the present earth, while others thought he would replace the old earth with a new one.** In your opinion, which model of the new heaven and earth seems to best fit the context of this passage? Explain.

2. John uses three metaphors to describe the new dwelling place of God and his people in verses 2-4. The first is "the Holy City, the new Jerusalem" (v. 2). What does this metaphor indicate about the nature of life in eternity?

3. John's second metaphor is "a bride beautifully dressed for her husband" (v. 2). Why is the marriage relationship a good analogy for our future life with Jesus Christ?

---

4. John's third metaphor moves from the more abstract "people" to that of a family (vv. 3, 7). How does the concept of a father living and caring for his children enrich your idea of eternity?

---

5. At the present time we live in a fallen world filled with pain and suffering. How can we take comfort from John's promise: "He will wipe every tear from their eyes. There will be no more death or mourning or crying or pain, for the old order of things has passed away" (v. 4)?

---

6. In John's Gospel Jesus cried out, "Let anyone who is thirsty come to me and drink" (John 7:37). How does his offer find its ultimate fulfillment in the new heaven and earth (v. 6)?

---

7. How does John make it clear that not everyone will experience the glorious future he describes (vv. 7-8)?

What contrasts does he make between the two groups in these verses?

---

8. After describing the heroes of faith in the Old Testament, the author of Hebrews wrote the following:

> All these people were still living by faith when they died. They did not receive the things promised; they only saw them and welcomed them from a distance, admitting that they were foreigners and strangers on earth. People who say such things show that they are looking for a country of their own. If they had been thinking of the country they had left, they would have had opportunity to return. Instead, they were longing for a better country—a heavenly one. Therefore God is not ashamed to be called their God, for he has prepared a city for them. (Hebrews 11:13-16)

How can the hope of the gospel give us the grace we need during our earthly pilgrimage?

Thank God for the amazing future he has promised us—both after death and when Jesus returns.

Now or Later

In what specific ways should our future hope in Christ affect the way we live each day on earth?

---

*Don Piper, *90 Minutes in Heaven* (Grand Rapids: Revell, 2004), 416-27.
**Craig S. Keener, *Revelation*, NIV Application Commentary (Grand Rapids: Zondervan, 2000), 485.

Leader's Notes

Leading a Bible discussion can be an enjoyable and rewarding experience. But it can also be *scary*—especially if you've never done it before. If this is your feeling, you're in good company. When God asked Moses to lead the Israelites out of Egypt, he replied, "Please send someone else" (Exodus 4:13)! It was the same with Solomon, Jeremiah, and Timothy, but God helped these people in spite of their weaknesses, and he will help you as well.

You don't need to be an expert on the Bible or a trained teacher to lead a Bible discussion. The idea behind these inductive studies is that the leader guides group members to discover for themselves what the Bible has to say. This method of learning will allow group members to remember much more of what is said than a lecture would.

These studies are designed to be led easily. As a matter of fact, the flow of questions through the passage from observation to interpretation to application is so natural that you may feel that the studies lead themselves. This study guide is also flexible. You can use it with a variety of groups—student, professional, neighborhood or church groups. Each study takes forty-five to sixty minutes in a group setting.

There are some important facts to know about group dynamics and encouraging discussion. The suggestions listed below should enable you to effectively and enjoyably fulfill your role as leader.

Preparing for the Study

1. Ask God to help you understand and apply the passage in your own life. Unless this happens, you will not be prepared to lead others. Pray too for the various members of the group. Ask God to open your hearts to the message of his Word and motivate you to action.

2. Read the introduction to the entire guide to get an overview of the entire book and the issues that will be explored.

3. As you begin each study, read and reread the assigned Bible passage to familiarize yourself with it.

4. This study guide is based on the New International Version of the Bible. It will help you and the group if you use this translation as the basis for your study and discussion.

5. Carefully work through each question in the study. Spend time in meditation and reflection as you consider how to respond.

6. Write your thoughts and responses in the space provided in the study guide. This will help you to express your understanding of the passage clearly.

7. It might help to have a Bible dictionary handy. Use it to look up any unfamiliar words, names, or places. (For additional help on how to study a passage, see chapter five of *How to Lead a LifeGuide Bible Study,* Inter-Varsity Press.)

8. Consider how you can apply the Scripture to your life. Remember that the group will follow your lead in responding to the studies. They will not go any deeper than you do.

9. Once you have finished your own study of the passage, familiarize yourself with the leader's notes for the study you are leading. These are designed to help you in several ways. First, they tell you the purpose the study guide author had in mind when writing the study. Take time to think through how the study questions work together to accomplish that purpose. Second, the notes provide you with additional background information or suggestions on group dynamics for various questions. This information can be useful when people have difficulty understanding or answering a question. Third, the leader's notes can alert you to potential problems you may encounter during the study.

10. If you wish to remind yourself of anything mentioned in the leader's notes, make a note to yourself below that question in the study.

Leading the Study

1. Begin the study on time. Open with prayer, asking God to help the group to understand and apply the passage.

2. Be sure that everyone in your group has a study guide. Encourage the group to prepare beforehand for each discussion by reading the introduction to the guide and by working through the questions in the study.

3. At the beginning of your first time together, explain that these studies are meant to be discussions, not lectures. Encourage the members of the group to participate. However, do not put pressure on those who may be hesitant to speak during the first few sessions. You may want to suggest the following guidelines to your group.

☐ Stick to the topic being discussed.

☐ Your responses should be based on the verses that are the focus of the discussion and not on outside authorities such as commentaries or speakers.

☐ These studies focus on a particular passage of Scripture. Only rarely should you refer to other portions of the Bible. This allows for everyone to participate in in-depth study on equal ground.

☐ Anything said in the group is considered confidential and will not be discussed outside the group unless specific permission is given to do so.

☐ We will listen attentively to each other and provide time for each person present to talk.

☐ We will pray for each other.

4. Have a group member read the introduction at the beginning of the discussion.

5. Every session begins with a group discussion question. The question or activity is meant to be used before the passage is read. The question introduces the theme of the study and encourages group members to begin to open up. Encourage as many members as possible to participate, and be ready to get the discussion going with your own response.

This section is designed to reveal where our thoughts or feelings need to be transformed by Scripture. That is why it is especially important not to read the passage before the discussion question is asked. The passage will tend to color the honest reactions people would otherwise give because they are, of course, supposed to think the way the Bible does.

You may want to supplement the group discussion question with an icebreaker to help people get comfortable. See the community section of *Small Group Idea Book* for more ideas.

You also might want to use the personal reflection question with your group. Either allow a time of silence for people to respond individually or discuss it together.

6. Have a group member (or members if the passage is long) read aloud the passage to be studied. Then give people several minutes to read the passage again silently so that they can take it all in.

7. Question 1 will generally be an overview question designed to briefly survey the passage. Encourage the group to look at the whole passage, but try to avoid getting sidetracked by questions or issues that will be addressed later in the study.

8. As you ask the questions, keep in mind that they are designed to be used just as they are written. You may simply read them aloud. Or you may prefer to express them in your own words.

There may be times when it is appropriate to deviate from the study guide. For example, a question may have already been answered. If so, move on to the next question. Or someone may raise an important question not covered in the guide. Take time to discuss it, but try to keep the group from going off on tangents.

9. Avoid answering your own questions. If necessary, repeat or rephrase them until they are clearly understood. Or point out something you read in the leader's notes to clarify the context or meaning. An eager group quickly becomes passive and silent if they think the leader will do most of the talking.

10. Don't be afraid of silence. People may need time to think about the question before formulating their answers.

11. Don't be content with just one answer. Ask, "What do the rest of you think?" or "Anything else?" until several people have given answers to the question.

12. Acknowledge all contributions. Try to be affirming whenever possible. Never reject an answer. If it is clearly off-base, ask, "Which verse led you to that conclusion?" or again, "What do the rest of you think?"

13. Don't expect every answer to be addressed to you, even though this will probably happen at first. As group members become more at ease, they will begin to truly interact with each other. This is one sign of healthy discussion.

14. Don't be afraid of controversy. It can be very stimulating. If you don't resolve an issue completely, don't be frustrated. Move on and keep it in mind for later. A subsequent study may solve the problem.

15. Periodically summarize what the group has said about the passage. This helps to draw together the various ideas mentioned and gives continuity to the study. But don't preach.

16. At the end of the Bible discussion you may want to allow group members a time of quiet to work on an idea under "Now or Later." Then discuss what you experienced. Or you may want to encourage group members to work on these ideas between meetings. Give an opportunity during the session for people to talk about what they are learning.

17. Conclude your time together with conversational prayer, adapting the prayer suggestion at the end of the study to your group. Ask for God's help in following through on the commitments you've made.

18. End on time.

Many more suggestions and helps are found in *How to Lead a Life-Guide Bible Study.*

Components of Small Groups

A healthy small group should do more than study the Bible. There are four components to consider as you structure your time together.

Nurture. Small groups help us to grow in our knowledge and love of God. Bible study is the key to making this happen and is the foundation of your small group.

Community. Small groups are a great place to develop deep friendships with other Christians. Allow time for informal interaction before and after each study. Plan activities and games that will help you get to know each other. Spend time having fun together going on a picnic or cooking dinner together.

Worship and prayer. Your study will be enhanced by spending time praising God together in prayer or song. Pray for each other's needs and keep track of how God is answering prayer in your group. Ask God to help you to apply what you are learning in your study.

Outreach. Reaching out to others can be a practical way of applying what you are learning, and it will keep your group from becoming self-focused. Host a series of evangelistic discussions for your friends or neighbors. Clean up the yard of an elderly friend. Serve at a soup kitchen together, or spend a day working on a Habitat house.

Many more suggestions and helps in each of these areas are found in *Small Group Idea Book*. Information on building a small group can be found in *Small Group Leaders' Handbook* and *The Big Book on Small Groups* (both from InterVarsity Press). Reading through one of these books would be worth your time.

Study 1. Created in His Image. Genesis 1:26–2:25.
Purpose: To realize that the sinful world around and within us is neither the original nor natural state God intended.
General note. You may wish to begin the study by reading aloud the introduction on page 9 or by summarizing its contents. If everyone has read it prior to the study, you can briefly go over the main points.
Question 2. *The Baker Illustrated Bible Dictionary* states, "That humankind has been created in the image of God indicates its unique status above the animals because of a special similarity with God. This status authorizes humankind to rule the earth and requires respect toward people" ("Image of God," in *The Baker Illustrated Bible Dictionary,* ed. Tremper Longman III [Grand Rapids: Baker, 2013], 826-27).
Question 4. Kenneth Kitchen writes,

> It is often claimed that Genesis 1 and 2 contain two different creation-narratives. In point of fact, however, the strictly *complementary* nature of the "two" accounts is plain enough: Genesis 1 mentions the creation of man as the last of a series, and without any details, whereas in Genesis 2 man is the centre of interest and more specific details are given about him and his setting. There is no incompatible duplication here at all. Failure to recognize the complementary nature of the subject-distinction between a skeleton outline of all creation on the one hand, and the concentration in detail on man and his immediate environment on the other, borders on obscurantism. (Kenneth Kitchen, *Ancient Orient and the Old Testament* [Downers Grove, IL: InterVarsity Press, 1975], 116-17)

Question 6. By placing the tree and its forbidden fruit in the middle of the Garden, the Lord gave Adam and Eve the freedom to choose whether to love and obey him or rebel against him. Without that choice, human freedom would not have been possible.
Question 8. Because God is by nature a relational being, he has created us to be in relationship with him and with others. Marriage is the most intimate human relationship on earth and most closely reflects the type of love experienced by the persons of the Trinity.

Study 2. The Fall of Humanity. Genesis 3.
Purpose: To look at "the dark threshold which, the account of the Fall says, man has crossed."

Questions 1-2. By asking, "Did God really say, 'You must not eat from any tree in the garden'?" the serpent is insinuating that God is far too strict and unreasonable. The woman replies with the statement, "We may eat fruit from the trees in the garden," even though the Lord had actually said, "You may *freely* eat the fruit of every tree in the garden" (NLT, emphasis added). Finally, the woman adds the words "you must not touch it," making God's command stricter than it really was. The serpent's words are like a poison that enters the woman's system and slowly alters her confidence in the Lord.

Question 3. The serpent is no longer subtle at this point but instead blatantly lies to the woman, "You won't die!" (NLT). Then he advances his argument even further when he states, "God knows that when you eat from it your eyes will be opened, and you will be like God, knowing good and evil." The serpent is trying to convince the woman that God does not have her best interests in mind but rather is deliberately keeping her from reaching her full potential.

Question 5. *The Baker Illustrated Bible Commentary* states the following:

> Verse 6 tells us that the temptation appealed, in the following order, to (1) Eve's physical appetites, (2) what she could see, and (3) her imagination. Note the thrust in this temptation. The serpent does not ask homage from Eve. Rather he indirectly suggests that she shift her commitment from doing God's will to doing her own will. (Victor P. Hamilton, "Genesis," in *The Baker Illustrated Bible Commentary*, ed. Gary M. Burge and Andrew E. Hill [Grand Rapids: Baker, 2012], 12)

Note the similarity of this temptation to John's words: "Everything in the world—the lust of the flesh, the lust of the eyes, and the pride of life—comes not from the Father but from the world" (1 John 2:16).

Question 7. The couple's responses to the Lord are a classic case of passing the buck. When the man says, "The woman you put here with me—she gave me some fruit from the tree, and I ate it," he is blaming not only the woman for his sin but also the Lord, who gave him the woman. The woman, in turn, blames the serpent when she says, "The serpent deceived me, and I ate." The serpent, of course, has no one left to blame and isn't given a chance to respond.

Question 10. The Bible does not evade the problem of evil but confronts it in the earliest chapters of the Bible, placing the blame on the couple's free choice, not on the Lord. In addition, C. S. Lewis writes,

> My argument against God was that the universe seemed so cruel
> and unjust. But how had I got this idea of "just" and "unjust"? . . .
> What was I comparing this universe with when I called it unjust?
> . . . Of course I could have given up my idea of justice by saying
> it was nothing but a private idea of my own. But if I did that,
> then my argument against God collapsed too—for the argument
> depended on saying that the world was really unjust, not simply
> that it did not happen to please my private fancies. .•. . Conse-
> quently atheism turns out to be too simple. (C. S. Lewis, *Mere
> Christianity* [San Francisco: HarperSanFrancisco, 2001], 38-39)

Study 3. The Call of Abram. Genesis 12:1-9.
Purpose: To look at the call of Abram and discover why he is such an
important part of the gospel narrative.
Questions 1-2. *The Baker Illustrated Bible Commentary* observes,

> God's first word to Abram is an imperative: leave! The three
> things he is to leave behind are arranged in ascending order:
> country, people, father's household. The imperative is followed
> by a series of promises relating to progeny, reputation, and bless-
> ing. . . . The climax of the divine "I wills" is that all peoples on
> earth (Genesis 10) will be blessed through Abram. Abram is to
> be not only a recipient of the blessing but also a channel through
> which this blessing may flow to others. (Victor P. Hamilton,
> "Genesis," in *The Baker Illustrated Bible Commentary*, ed. Gary
> M. Burge and Andrew E. Hill [Grand Rapids: Baker, 2012], 22)

Question 3. John Walton writes,

> I propose that the nature of the blessing on the nations is that
> God has revealed himself through Abram's family. The law was
> given through them; the prophets were from among their num-
> ber; Scripture was written by them; and their history became
> a public record of God's attributes in action. Then to climax it
> all, his own Son came through them and revealed the Father
> and the kingdom through his life and a plan of salvation for the
> world through his death. In Abram all the nations of the earth
> were blessed as they were shown what God was like and as the
> means were provided for them to become justified, reconciled

to God, and forgiven of their sins. (John H. Walton, *Genesis*, NIV Application Commentary [Grand Rapids: Zondervan, 2001], 402)

Question 6. The apostle Paul gives us the best commentary on Abram's faith:

Against all hope, Abraham in hope believed and so became the father of many nations, just as it had been said to him, "So shall your offspring be." Without weakening in his faith, he faced the fact that his body was as good as dead—since he was about a hundred years old—and that Sarah's womb was also dead. Yet he did not waver through unbelief regarding the promise of God, but was strengthened in his faith and gave glory to God, being fully persuaded that God had power to do what he had promised. (Romans 4:18-21)

Question 7. In verse 7 the Lord promises Abram, "To your offspring I will give this land." But when Abram arrives in the Promised Land, it is occupied by the Canaanites, and the conquest of the land will not take place until the time of Joshua, long after Abram has died. The author of Hebrews writes, "By faith Abraham, when called to go to a place he would later receive as his inheritance, obeyed and went, even though he did not know where he was going. By faith he made his home in the promised land like a stranger in a foreign country; he lived in tents" (Hebrews 11:8-9).

Question 9. Rather than wavering in faith or being discouraged about the occupation of the land by the Canaanites, Abram repeatedly builds altars to the Lord, expressing his confidence in the One who called him.

Study 4. The Law of Moses. Deuteronomy 6.

Purpose: To help us affirm and appreciate the goodness of God's commands.

Question 1. Daniel I. Block writes,

The proper human disposition before the glorious and gracious God remains fear, the deep sense of awe in his presence, which alone will produce acceptable liturgical response and the worship of daily obedience. Where there is no fear, there is no sense of obligation and no sense of gratitude that we have stood in the presence of God and lived to tell about it. Without fear, the privileged life of obedience is reduced to a burdensome duty. (Daniel I. Block, *Deuteronomy*, NIV Application Commentary [Grand Rapids: Zondervan, 2012], 179)

Question 3. The love commands in the Bible include the following: "Love the LORD your God with all your heart and with all your soul and with all your strength" (Deuteronomy 6:5); "love your neighbor as yourself" (Leviticus 19:18); and "Love one another. As I have loved you, so you must love one another" (John 13:34). These great commandments reveal that love, which expresses itself in the kind of sacrificial service that Jesus demonstrated on the cross, is at the heart of every command in God's Word.

Why then were over six hundred commands of the Old Testament necessary? They were needed to define and illustrate what it means to love in the specific situations of everyday life. For example, what did it mean to love your neighbor in business practices? "Do not use dishonest standards when measuring length, weight or quantity" (Leviticus 19:35). What did it mean to love those who were hungry and needy? "When you reap the harvest of your land, do not reap to the very edges of your field or gather the gleanings of your harvest. . . . Leave them for the poor and the foreigner" (Leviticus 19:9-10).

Question 4. Daniel I. Block says,

Moses taught his people and he teaches us and Christians everywhere that true spirituality arises from the heart and extends to all of life. Those who claim to be religious tend to be subject to two temptations: either to treat spirituality as primarily interior and private, or to treat it as a matter of external performance. True love for God is rooted in the heart, but it is demonstrated in life, specifically a passion to speak of one's faith in the context of the family and to declare one's allegiance publicly to the world. (Block, *Deuteronomy*, 189)

Question 6. The author of Proverbs 30:8-9 tells the Lord,

Give me neither poverty nor riches,
    but give me only my daily bread.
Otherwise, I may have too much and disown you
    and say, "Who is the Lord?"
Or I may become poor and steal,
    and so dishonor the name of my God.

Question 7. The saints of the Old Testament looked back to the exodus, where God delivered his people from slavery through his mighty power, as proof that they were his covenant people. This defining moment in the life of the nation served as a reminder of God's faithfulness in the present. In the same way, Christians in the New Testament looked back on the crucifixion and resurrection of Jesus as the clearest demonstration of God's everlasting love and commitment to his children.

Study 5. The Power of Sin. Romans 3:9-20.

Purpose: To discover why we must accept the Bible's diagnosis of our condition before we can experience healing grace.

Question 1. Notice Paul's sweeping language in these verses:

> There is *no one* righteous, *not even one*;
>> there is *no one* who understands,
>> there is *no one* who seeks God.
> *All* have turned away,
>> they have *together* become worthless;
> there is *no one* who does good,
>> *not even one*. (Romans 3:10-12, emphasis added)

Question 2. This question begins with the statement, "There are billions of religious people throughout the world." There are over one billion Muslims in the world, over 750 million Hindus, nearly 334 million Buddhists, and around 16 million Jews. Paul is claiming that out of the nearly four billion religious people on earth, not even one of them is righteous.

Question 4. Quoting from various Old Testament passages, Paul writes,

> "Their *throats* are open graves;
>> their *tongues* practice deceit."
> "The poison of vipers is on their *lips*."
>> "Their *mouths* are full of cursing and bitterness."
> "Their *feet* are swift to shed blood. . . ."
>> "There is no fear of God before their *eyes*." (Romans 3:13-18, emphasis added)

In other words, sin has infected every part of us—throats, tongues, lips, mouths, feet, eyes—but also our minds, our hearts, our will. Theologians call this "total depravity." They don't mean that we have all become as bad as we could be. We're not all Adolf Hitlers, Charles Mansons, or Jeffery Dahmers. But every part of us has been infected and corrupted by sin.

Questions 5-6. According to Paul, our problem is not simply that we sin but that we are sinful. In other words, sin goes deeper than actions, deeper than behavior—all the way to our hearts.

You cannot simply tell a non-Christian to "stop sinning" any more than you can tell someone with the flu to stop running a fever. Because sin has affected us like a cancer, it requires a radical solution— a miraculous cure—that can only be accomplished by Jesus' death on the cross and the gift of the Holy Spirit.

Question 7. Paul says in verses 19-20 that on the Judgment Day the evidence against humanity will be so enormous that it will be impossible to protest. Instead, "every mouth [will] be silenced" and the whole world will be "held accountable to God." The Bible says there is universal guilt, and there will be universal condemnation.

Of course, the Bible could have ended with this message. God could have sent a prophet like Paul to tell us that we have sinned, we are guilty, we will be condemned, and will experience God's wrath on Judgment Day.

We sometimes wonder whether God is unjust for not saving everyone. The fact is that he would be perfectly just not to save anyone! That is the message of Romans 1:18–3:20.

The fact that the Bible does go on, and that God sent his only Son to be our Savior, is not something that we deserve or that his justice demanded. It is a pure act of grace, love, and mercy.

Study 6. The Gift of Righteousness. Romans 3:21-31.
Purpose: To understand the meaning of the "righteousness of God" that comes through faith in Jesus Christ.
Question 1. Tom Schreiner writes,

> From 1:18 to 3:20 Paul has argued that all people deserve God's wrath and judgment. Not even the covenant people are an exception, since they have failed to keep the Mosaic law. Indeed, the burden of 2:1-29, which is summed up in 3:19-20, is that the Mosaic law provides no power for obedience. The law only reveals the transgressions of both Jews and Gentiles. Thus reliance on the law or on Jewish distinctives is a false path. Romans 3:21-26 turns the corner in the argument.

The saving righteousness of God is not available through the law, but has been revealed in Jesus Christ and his atoning death. The promises made to Israel have been fulfilled, but they have been fulfilled in a surprising way—through the death of Jesus on the cross. Those who put their faith in him are thereby right with God. (Thomas R. Schreiner, *Romans*, Baker Exegetical Commentary on the New Testament [Grand Rapids: Baker Academic, 1998], 178)

Question 3. Justification according to Paul is more than simply being forgiven or having our guilt removed. In addition, we are clothed in the righteousness of Jesus Christ—a righteousness that is not our own but rather a gift of God.

Question 4. Marvin Pate observes,

In Romans 3:24, Paul says, "All are justified freely by his grace through the redemption that came by Christ Jesus." The Greek word translated "redemption" was used to describe the process by which slaves could purchase their freedom. In Roman culture, slaves could be freed in several ways. They could be freed directly by their masters, or they could earn money (the equivalent of their purchase price) to eventually buy their freedom. Free men might purchase the freedom of female slaves in order to marry them. Freed slaves then had the status of *libertus* (freedman) or *liberta* (freedwoman). (C. Marvin Pate, *Romans*, Teach the Text Commentary [Grand Rapids: Baker, 2013], 78)

Question 6. The word translated as "sacrifice of atonement" (v. 25) is the same word used to describe the "mercy seat," which was the lid of the ark of the covenant. So in what sense has Jesus become like the mercy seat for us?

The ark of the covenant was inside the most sacred place in the temple—the Holy of Holies—where God manifested his presence in a special way. Once a year the high priest would enter this room, which was hidden behind a thick curtain, and sprinkle the blood of a sacrificial animal for his own sins and the sins of the people. In Leviticus 16:15-16 the Lord says:

[Aaron] shall then slaughter the goat for the sin offering for the people and take its blood behind the curtain and do with it as he did with the bull's blood: He shall sprinkle it on the atonement cover and in front of it. In this way he will make atonement for the Most Holy Place because of the uncleanness and rebellion of the Israelites, whatever their sins have been.

According to the New Testament, Christ's violent death on the cross (which is what Paul means by "his blood") satisfied the justice of God and turned away his wrath from us forever—if we have faith in Jesus and what he has done for us.

Question 7. God's justice demands that those who sin be punished. But his love desires that people be saved from their sins. These two attributes appear on the surface to cancel out each other, but at the cross they are brought together in perfect harmony. God's justice is satisfied through the death of his Son on the cross, and his grace and mercy toward sinners is also affirmed by offering the way of salvation as a free gift by faith in Christ.

Study 7. Transformed by the Spirit. 2 Corinthians 3:7-18.
Purpose: To grasp God's promise that we are being transformed into his likeness by the Holy Spirit, and that one day we will be as pure and radiant as Jesus himself.

Question 1. Paul is not claiming that the old covenant had no glory—quite the contrary. He is using an argument from the lesser to the greater, claiming that since the old covenant had glory then the new covenant must have a far greater glory.

Question 2. In order to understand this passage, we need to look at its Old Testament background. After Moses received the Ten Commandments from the Lord and descended Mount Sinai, his face was radiant with the glory of God. When Aaron and all the Israelites saw Moses' face, they were afraid to come near him. So Moses put a veil over his face whenever he was with the Israelites, but when he went back into the "tent of meeting," where he met with the Lord, he took off the veil (see Exodus 34:29-35).

Paul adds something the Old Testament does not explain: when Moses left the presence of the Lord, the glory in his face began to fade, but when he was in the Lord's presence, the glory increased.

Question 4. Moses only uncovered his face when he was in the presence of the Lord, and he covered it when he left the Lord's presence. When Paul says our faces are always unveiled, he is saying, in essence, that we are always in the Lord's presence—not just once a year or even once a day. We dwell permanently in the presence of the Almighty, and he dwells in us through his Spirit. As members of the body of Christ, the church, we have become the Holy of Holies—the temple of the Lord.

Question 5. In the beginning, humanity was created in the image and likeness of God himself (Genesis 1:26-27). For centuries theologians have discussed and debated what this means. However, one thing is clear: the fact that humanity was already in God's image made the incarnation of Jesus Christ possible. There was such a correspondence between God and humanity that he could become a human forever and still be able to fully reveal God's character and glory. After the fall, the image of God in humanity was defaced, but through Christ it is being fully restored by the Spirit. Therefore, one day we too will reflect the character and glory of God.

Questions 6-7. A note on 2 Corinthians 3:18 in the ESV Study Bible says,

> As a result of beholding the Lord through the ministry of the Spirit, the believer is being transformed (a process of sanctification over time, not an instantaneous change) into the same image of God that was distorted at the fall (see Gen. 1:26-27; 2 Cor. 4:4; 5:17; also 1 John 3:2). The "image" of God includes every way in which humans are like God, such as their moral character, their true knowledge, their many God-given abilities, and their dominion over creation (cf. Gen. 1:26-28), to be exercised with dependence on God as the Creator and giver of all things (see 1 Cor. 4:7). (ESV Study Bible [Wheaton, IL: Crossway, 2008])

Question 8. Pastor Tom Steller writes about the end of our journey, when we will finally see Jesus Christ and become fully like him:

> This sight of Jesus is going to be so stunning, so real, so breathtaking, so irresistible. All the fog in our vision will be burned away by the noon day brightness of his glory. We're going to see once and for all how ridiculous it was to have been enamored by the fleeting pleasures of sin. The lust of the flesh, the lust of the eyes, and the pride of life are going to appear as gravel in comparison to his diamond-studded brilliance.
>
> And this beholding of Jesus in all his glory will prove irresistible. It's going to swallow us up. We are going to be transformed into his likeness, irresistibly. Not that we are going to be forced against our will to be like Jesus. We won't be able

to resist it because we won't want to. Our admiration of him will be so total that all other competing role models will be left in the dust. (Tom Steller, "We Shall Be Like Him," *Sound of Grace*, accessed May 17, 2016, www.soundofgrace.com/piper85/ pn850011.htm)

Study 8. The Resurrection. 1 Corinthians 15:1-33.
Purpose: To understand why the resurrection of Jesus is one of the central components of the gospel.
Question 2. Craig Blomberg writes,

"That Christ died" (v. 3) refutes those docetists who believed that Christ only seemed to be human (because they also believed that matter was inherently evil). That it was "for our sins" points to a vicarious atonement—paying the penalty we deserved to pay on our behalf. "According to the Scriptures" probably has in mind passages such as those in Isaiah 52–53 that speak of God's suffering servant. Jesus' burial (v. 4) again certifies that he really died and also points forward to the empty tomb and the reality of the resurrection. "On the third day" uses inclusive reckoning: Good Friday is day one, Saturday is day two, and Easter morning is day three. It is less clear which Scriptures point to the resurrection on the third day. Perhaps Paul meant only that the Scriptures testified to Christ's resurrection, with passages like Psalms 16:8-11 and 110:1-4 in view (cf. Acts 2:24- 36). (Craig Blomberg, *1 Corinthians*, NIV Application Commentary [Grand Rapids: Zondervan, 1994], 296)

Question 3. Commenting on the resurrection witnesses, William Lillie writes,

What gives a special authority to the list [of witnesses] as historical evidence is the reference to most of the five hundred brethren being still alive. St. Paul says in effect, "If you do not believe me, you can ask them." Such a statement in an admittedly genuine letter written within thirty years of the event is almost as strong evidence as one could hope to get for something that happened nearly two thousand years ago. (William Lillie, quoted in Edwin M. Yamauchi, "Easter: Myth, Hallucination, or History?," LeaderU.com, March 15, 1974, www.leaderu .com/everystudent/easter/articles/yama.html)

Question 4. Paul tells us that if there is no resurrection of the dead, then (1) "not even Christ has been raised," (2) "our preaching is useless and so is your faith," (3) "we are then found to be false witnesses about God," (4) "your faith is futile," (5) "you are still in your sins," (6) "those also who have fallen asleep in Christ are lost," (7) "we are of all people most to be pitied," (8) there is no point in people being baptized, (9) there is no reason for Paul and others to endanger themselves by preaching the gospel, and (10) life itself is futile (v. 32).

Don't take much time to discuss Paul's enigmatic statement about being baptized for the dead. There has been a lot of speculation about what he meant, but most commentators admit that we simply don't know.

A note in the NIV Study Bible on 1 Corinthians 15:29 states,

Those . . . who are baptized for the dead. The present tense suggests that at Corinth people were currently being baptized for the dead. But because Paul does not give any more information about the practice, many attempts have been made to interpret the concept. Three of these are: (1) Living believers were being baptized for believers who died before they were baptized, so that they too, in this way, would not miss out on baptism. (2) Christians were being baptized in anticipation of the resurrection of the dead. (3) New converts were being baptized to fill the ranks of Christians who had died. At any rate, Paul mentions this custom almost in passing, using it in his arguments substantiating the resurrection of the dead but without necessarily approving the practice. The passage will likely remain obscure.

Question 7. Many Christians today give little thought to either the resurrection or the fact that we will live on a new earth. Instead, their vision of eternity is that they will live "in heaven" with Jesus in a disembodied state. These beliefs are similar to those of the Corinthians, who were influenced by Greek philosophy that taught the immortality of the soul but denied the resurrection, since the body was evil. In contrast, Jesus and the apostles affirmed the goodness of creation by emphasizing that we will spend eternity in resurrected bodies on a renewed earth.

Study 9. Heaven on Earth. Revelation 21:1-8.
Purpose: To discover what life will be like after Jesus returns and we live with him in the "new heaven and a new earth."
Question 2. *The Baker Illustrated Bible Dictionary* comments,

> Both Ezekiel and Revelation envision a new Jerusalem and use similar imagery to describe it and to emphasize God's presence in the city (Ezek. 48:30-35; Rev. 21:1–22:5). According to Revelation, the throne of God, the Lamb, and the river of life are present in the new Jerusalem, which comes down from heaven, is made of gold and glass, is adorned with jewels, and is in the shape of a cube. Only those with names in the Lamb's book of life will dwell in the city (Rev. 21:27). The city represents a new, spiritual order (Gal. 4:25-26; Heb. 12:22). ("New Jerusalem," in *The Baker Illustrated Bible Dictionary*, ed. Tremper Longman III [Grand Rapids: Baker, 2013], 1211)

The city also emphasizes the fact that believers will live in community with God and each other.
Question 3. *The Baker Illustrated Bible Commentary* says,

> As John witnesses the descent of a new and more glorious Jerusalem on the earth, he is reminded by the angelic intermediary that the city is the bride of the Lamb. Despite the complexity of the building metaphors used to describe the New Jerusalem, it is not a place but a people (21:9-10; cf. Isa. 64:17-19). John's panoramic overview of the whole city has one central theme: the deep and permanent communion of God with the church. (Max J. Lee, "Revelation," in *The Baker Illustrated Bible Commentary*, ed. Gary M. Burge and Andrew E. Hill [Grand Rapids: Baker, 2012], 1626)

Marriage is the most intimate relationship possible here on earth, since "the two become one flesh"—an experience that Paul says applies to Christ and the church (Ephesians 5:31-32).
Question 5. One of the most difficult aspects of living in a fallen world is the experience of suffering, hardship, pain, and even death. But John makes it clear that these things—and the tears that accompany them—will no longer be part of our lives in the new heaven and the new earth.
Question 6. In John's Gospel Jesus tells the woman at the well that "whoever drinks the water I give them will never thirst. Indeed, the water I give them will become in them a spring of water welling up to

eternal life" (John 4:14). He also made the offer at the Festival of Tabernacles, "Let anyone who is thirsty come to me and drink. Whoever believes in me, as Scripture has said, rivers of living water will flow from within them" (John 7:37-38). John explains to his readers, "By this he meant the Spirit, whom those who believed in him were later to receive. Up to that time the Spirit had not been given, since Jesus had not yet been glorified" (v. 39). In Revelation 21:6 Jesus tells us, "To the thirsty I will give water without cost from the spring of the water of life." We need to keep in mind that whether Jesus is referring to a well, a river, or a spring, he is ultimately speaking of himself and the life-giving Spirit of God.

Question 7. John promises that "those who are victorious will inherit all this, and I will be their God and they will be my children" (v. 7). But he also makes it clear that "the cowardly, the unbelieving, the vile, the murderers, the sexually immoral, those who practice magic arts, the idolaters and all liars—they will be consigned to the fiery lake of burning sulfur. This is the second death" (v. 8). People have interpreted "the fiery lake of burning sulfur" in a variety of ways. But the Bible clearly teaches that God is the source of life, and that separation from him results in both physical and spiritual death.

Jack Kuhatschek was formerly executive vice president and publisher for Baker Publishing Group, Grand Rapids, Michigan. He is the author of many Bible study guides and the books Applying the Bible *and* The Superman Syndrome. *He and his wife, Sandy, currently live in Deland, Florida.*

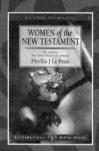

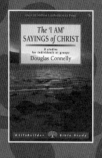
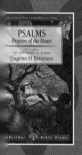
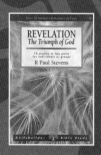